Dig a Pit

Written by Caroline Green

Collins

It can dig.

It gets up on top.

It sets off.

It dips and pulls in the hot sun.

It digs up the muck.

It is a big pit!

It pulls up mud and rocks.

It is full.

It tips the rocks on top.

Men put rocks in and fill sacks.
It picks up the sacks.

It puts the sacks on top.

/r/

14

🐾 Review: After reading 🐾

Use your assessment from hearing the children read to choose any GPCs, words or tricky words that need additional practice.

Read 1: Decoding

- Reread pages 4 and 5 and ask the children to mime the digger's actions with their arm and hand. Point to these words while the children mime the action:

  sets off (*arm moves along*)   **dips** (*hand dips down*)   **pulls** (*hand comes up, tugging*)

- Ensure the children can read words ending in "s" successfully. Ask the children to turn to pages 2 and 3. Show them how to read the word **gets** by covering up the "s", reading the word "get" and then adding the "s" to read the whole word **gets**.

- Turn to pages 12 and 13. Point to the following, saying: Blend in your head when you read these words:

  Men   **rocks**   **fill**   **picks**   **sacks**   **top**

- Look at the "I spy sounds" pages (14–15) together. How many objects can the children point out and name that start with the /r/ sound? (e.g. *rabbit, rocks, rake, rope, ruler, radio, raspberries, rubber, rat*)

Read 2: Prosody

- Read page 12 together. Ask: What is **It**? (*the digger, not the men*) Say: Let's read the page, emphasising **It**, so a listener knows we don't mean the men.

- Encourage the children to read pages 12 and 13, emphasising the pronoun on each.

Read 3: Comprehension

- Ask the children if they have seen any diggers. Ask: Was it like this digger? Where did you see it?

- Ask: What sort of book is this – a story book? (*No, it's a non-fiction book.*) What have you learnt from it? (e.g. *what a digger can do*)

- Look through the book, and ask:

  o Pages 6 and 7: What is the digger doing? (e.g. *digging up the muck to make a big pit*)

  o Pages 10 and 11: Is it still digging? (*No, it is tipping rocks.*)

  o Pages 12 and 13: Is it tipping things now? (*No, it is picking up sacks.*)